31 DAYS TO A GREATER UNDERSTANDING OF
MONEY

Biblical Principles to Help You Get Out of Debt & Enjoy the Life God Has For You

D1081919

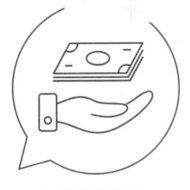

MASTER FINANCIAL COACH
KAREN FORD

Copyright © 2017 Karen Ford

31 Days to a Greater Understanding of MONEY

Printed in the USA

Published by KBF Management Company, Fairmont, WV

Prepared for publication by www.wendykwalters.com

ISBN (print) : 978-0-9995415-0-0
ISBN (kindle): 978-0-9995415-1-7
Library of Congress Control Number (LCCN): 2017957956

Presented To:

MCPLS

By:

Karen Ford

Special thanks to
Joe, my husband,
for being so patient
with me throughout
this process.
Your support means
the world to me.

WHAT OTHERS ARE SAYING

Karen Ford is one who not only lives what she writes, but who also lives to impart to others experienced truths that have brought her into financial freedom. These daily devotions not only impart practical knowledge, but also wisdom as to how to apply these truths. The questions offered will provoke personal evaluation that will open the readers' eyes to habits in their lives and challenge them to make better decisions in their lives!

—DR. REBECCA POLIS
COACH, TEACHER
CO-FOUNDER OF FAITH CHURCH INTERNATIONAL

Karen is a dutiful, faithful servant who takes economic lessons from the Bible and presents them in an easy to understand forum to help you get out of debt to enjoy the life that God wants you to have.

—DOUG WHITE
CEO BDW MANAGEMENT INC
CFO MALACHI 310 INVESTMENTS, LLC

Karen Ford's book, *31 Days to a Greater Understanding of MONEY,* is as inspirational as it is practical. Each day's devotion wraps you in God's love for you and brings you into a mindset of more than enough, abundance, and overflow.

—WENDY K. WALTERS
ENTREPRENEUR, BRANDING & PUBLISHING EXPERT

CONTENTS

FOREWORD by Dr. John Polis 1

Day 1 - Be Like the Ant 3

Day 2 - Where Are Your Thoughts? 7

Day 3 - Have You Landed? 11

Day 4 - It Just Takes a Little 15

Day 5 - Knowing is Key 19

Day 6 - What's in Your Hand? 21

Day 7 - What Do You Want? 23

Day 8 - Trust in Him 25

Day 9 - Take No Thought Saying 27

Day 10 - What's in Your House? 31

Day 11 - What Are You Saying? 35

Day 12 - Contentment 39

Day 13 - Give From the Heart 41

Day 14 - Lend and Rule 43

Day 15 - It's Open 45

Day 16 - Rule or Be Ruled 47

Day 17 - What Should You Owe? 49

Day 18 - How to Give 53

Day 19 - Are You SURE About Surety? 57

Day 20 - Will of the Heart   59

Day 21 - Honor   63

Day 22 - Generosity   67

Day 23 - Blessed   71

Day 24 - Open Windows   75

Day 25 - How to Give   77

Day 26 - Now is the Time   81

Day 27 - Work Method   83

Day 28 - Grace   85

Day 29 - Sow   87

Day 30 - Reap   91

Day 31 - Gifts   95

CONCLUSION   99

FOREWORD BY DR. JOHN POLIS

Karen Ford is an amazing woman with a fierce determination to walk in all the spoils of Christ's work on the Cross. For more than twenty years, I have had the privilege of not only serving as her employer and pastor, but also as a co-worker and friend. She is an ordained elder and also serves as the administrator for Faith Church International.

As a Certified Financial Coach after years of practicing and proving the principles she teaches, Karen has a proven record of helping people successfully reach their financial goals. She not only provides the information and tools to achieve financial freedom, but she is also a role model of applying biblical wisdom to both business and personal finance. I am confident this devotional will be a resource you will want to read again and again.

—DR. JOHN POLIS
PRESIDENT, REVIVAL FELLOWSHIP INTERNATIONAL, INC.
SR.PASTOR, FAITH CHURCH INTERNATIONAL

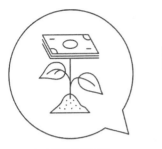

DAY 1

Be Like the Ant

> *Go to the ant, sluggard; consider her ways and be wise; who having no guide, overseer, or ruler, provides her food in the summer and gathers her food in the harvest.*
>
> PROVERBS 6:6-8 KJV

The ant is an interesting creature and we can certainly learn from its abilities how we should work.

First, let's look at how we are not to be. The verse mentions a sluggard.

A sluggard is lazy, loves to stay in bed and doesn't like to work. He is too arrogant to be teachable. In Proverbs 6, Solomon was comparing sluggards to ants when he said, "Go to the ant and consider her ways."

The word "ways" means "road" and is symbolic of a course of life. We are to observe the ant's course of life and direction.

Ants never quit! They are persistent. When they are looking for food, they don't allow any obstacle to get in their way. They don't give up until they reach their goal. They are always moving and don't need supervision! They confront their obstacles and go around them or over them or through them until they have achieved their desired outcomes.

Ants aren't intimidated by the sheer size of the objects they need to carry, so why should we?

We should be a people who never quit, not allowing any real or perceived obstacle to get in our way.

The ant is a primary example of diligence. The word "diligence" means "a determined and earnest effort." Ants are determined to attain the achievement they have before them. There is a reward for diligence. "He that comes to God, must believe that He is and that He is a rewarder of those who diligently seek Him."

Let's be like the ant that never gives up on its goal—they persist.

In the summertime ants think winter. They gather and store food for the times when food will be scarce. They stay underground during the winter season consuming the food stored up during the prosperity of summer. Without any rulers, guides, or overseers, ants are conscious of the future and prepare for it.

They are hard workers, self-starters and they don't need a sergeant to get them started or keep them going. They save for the future. When things are going well for us (summer), we should be planning for the times when things may go wrong. We need to prepare ourselves today with skills that we will need in the future.

Prepare yourself today with skills you will need in your future

Jim Rohn was a man many considered to be America's Business Philosopher and a question he would ask is, "How much does an ant gather during summer to prepare for winter?" The answer, "All that he possibly can!"

Do All That You Can

- If you want to have a great marriage—do all that you can!
- If you want to raise confident children—do all that you can!
- If you want to be empowered—do all that you can!
- If you want to have a great career—do all that you can!
- If you want to have great relationships—do all that you can!
- If you want to be prosperous—do all that you can!

God rewards action. Think like an ant and strive like an ant!

Lord, I see in your Word how the ant works and strives to be prepared. I ask that you help me to be more diligent with my activities throughout the day. Help me to be one that perseveres to reach the goals you have placed before me. Amen.

---

persist

to go on resolutely
in spite of
opposition; to
remain fixed

DAY 2

Where Are Your Thoughts?

> *The plans of the diligent lead only to plenty, but everyone who is hasty comes only to poverty.*
>
> PROVERBS 21:5 NET

Solomon often compares two different kinds of people. In this proverb, he is describing a diligent man who gets rich and a hasty man who becomes poor.

The word hasty in the Scriptures is almost always attached to poverty.

The hasty person doesn't think before he acts. He's a person who doesn't think over a matter and the possible consequences. The thought enters his head and he acts on it without thinking beforehand. This leads to poverty because he may execute the act even if it's unwise or unjust.

A "hasty" person is a person who hears about a "great deal" (investments or sales), and just jumps in and goes for it before weighing the risks or considering the potential problems that could arise.

Because we are people of faith, we base our decisions upon the Word. Isaiah 28:16b (KJV) says, "He that believeth shall not make haste."

We are to think before we act!

Diligence is the key to wealth!

The diligent person thinks on how they will work and accomplish the tasks at hand.

The diligent person plans their work and works his plans.

Webster's dictionary defines diligence as "attentive, persistent, constant in effort to accomplish something." So, diligence is a person who takes steady steps toward executing a carefully laid out plan. This doesn't mean that they are in a sprint, but rather, a marathon. He isn't motivated to get to the goal as quickly as possible, but to get to the goal, period. They are diligent by moving forward and they "keep on keeping on." He isn't looking for a quick reward or "get rich quick" scheme. Those who are diligent to work and invest time will reap the reward of plenty.

The diligent will pursue and press onward

Although there may be times of challenge and difficulty, the diligent will pursue and press onward.

A great example of diligence in the Bible is Joseph. Although he was sold into slavery by his brothers and was taken to Egypt, he developed that quality of diligence. When he was sold as a slave to Potiphar, Joseph worked with diligence.

As a result, Potiphar entrusted him with added responsibility and before long, Joseph was handling everything in the estate. Diligence changed his circumstances.

Are we diligent in carrying out the requests by our boss, our mate, those who we serve with diligence?

This Scripture also mentions thoughts of the diligent and thoughts of the hasty. They both have thoughts! Why does one end up with plenty and one in poverty? Our thoughts form our habits and we become our habits. "As a man thinketh in his heart, so is he." We can align ourselves to plenty (wealth) with our thoughts of perseverance and accomplishments.

When we are diligent—purposed to keep taking steps, executing the plans—this will lead to plenty (wealth).

What are you thinking about?

Lord, I ask that you help me today so that I can have the right thoughts of diligence to do all that you will have me to do. Lord, I need you to help me so that like Joseph, even if I am treated less than I deserve, that I will still be diligent to do what you have called me to do. Amen.

---

diligence

steady, earnest,
and energetic
effort; persevering
application

DAY 3

Have You Landed?

> *He who tills his land will have plenty of food, but he who*
> *follows empty pursuits will have poverty in plenty.*
>
> PROVERBS 28:19 NASB

A person who follows empty pursuits is one who is usually found pursuing the get-rich-quick schemes. The word "empty" in this verse means "the pursuit amounts to nothing." Following empty pursuits is what leads one to poverty.

It reminds me of the passage that reads, "I went by the field of the slothful, and the vineyard of the man void of understanding, and I saw and considered it well. I looked upon it and received instruction. A little sleep, a little slumber, a little folding of the hands to sleep and your want cometh as one that traveleth and your poverty as an armed man" (Prov 24:30-34 KJV).

See, the one who doesn't work, or pursues things that are empty, will lead them to poverty.

But, God is saying that those who till their ground (work) will have plenty. He is saying one is to work, and to work hard.

This Scripture illustrates work! Farming was not the only job in Solomon's day, but it is used to illustrate that people who work will have plenty. Farming is work and it can be hard, challenging, but the reward is that we end up with plenty. Farming and all types of work require integrity, responsibility, commitment, quality and discipline.

- Integrity fosters relationships of trust with coworkers, customers, and supervisors.

- Your coworkers will value your honest feedback.

- Customers trust your advice.

- Supervisors know they can trust you because of your integrity.

- Responsibility affects how you work and the amount of work you do. When you take responsibility for your performance, you will be on time for work, give your best effort, and will complete work on time.

- Commitment means you will do the work that is required of you, though you may not enjoy every aspect, you're committed to the work at hand.

- Quality of work means you do your best to produce great work and not just do what is needed to get by. You will go the extra mile and go above and beyond.

- Discipline will cause you to stay focused on your goals and complete tasks on time.

- When tilling land (working), it requires integrity, responsibility, commitment, quality, and discipline.

The Message Translation of today's scripture is this: "Work your garden—you'll end up with plenty of food; play and party—you'll end up with an empty plate." When we work we are rewarded with plenty. Are you setting yourself up for plenty?

Father, I ask that you help me to be a good worker, that I will be a person of integrity who has gained trust. I ask that my work reflect that I am responsible, disciplined, and committed to carry out the tasks and assignments of the day. Lord, let the quality of my work be a reflection of you. Amen.

---

integrity

the quality of
being honest and
having strong
moral principles;
moral uprightness

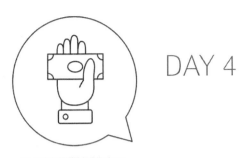

DAY 4

It Just Takes a Little

> *"He who is faithful in a very little thing is faithful also in much; and he who is unrighteous in a very little thing is unrighteous also in much."*
>
> LUKE 16:10 NASB

This scripture teaches us that whether we have more or less, we are to be faithful. Those who use gifts unfaithfully will be unfaithful in spiritual matters. In other words, if we don't use our gifts and temporal things for the glory of God, we most likely won't use them for the Kingdom.

You might wonder or even ask, "How do I know if I am faithful?"

Here are some questions for you to consider:

- Do others have to remind you to get things done?
- Do you return phone calls?
- Do you keep your word or are you flimsy with it?

The word faithful is the Greek word "pistos" and means "sure, true, and trustworthy." This is a person that will do what he says and carry out the task with great excellence in a timely manner.

I've heard some say, "I'll be more faithful with money when I get more."

My response is, "No, you won't." Why? Because if you're not faithful with little you won't be faithful with more.

Great opportunities disguise themselves as small tasks

Our faithfulness in the little will determine how we will be with more.

This is applicable to every area of life.

Great opportunities disguise themselves as small tasks.

These are character building occasions.

If I have an employee that isn't faithful with carrying out the assignment when and how I have instructed, then why would I give that employee more responsibility?

Make these commitments today and daily confess over your life and walk with God.

- I will be faithful in the little things, so I will be faithful in much.

- As I am faithful in little, God will entrust me with more.

- I will be faithful with the amount of money I have now, so God can trust me with more.

Lord, I ask that you help me use the gifts, talents, and money that you have given me to the best I can. I ask that you help me to be more faithful, and as I become more faithful, you will not only give me more, but you will help me be faithful in the much. Amen.

faithful

loyal, constant,
staunch, steadfast,
resolute

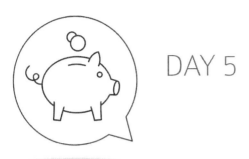

DAY 5

Knowing is Key

> *Know well the state of your flocks; and pay attention to your herds.*
>
> PROVERBS 27:23 NASB

The word "know" means "to acknowledge, to be aware, and to ascertain by seeing." We are to be keenly aware of what is going on.

When you think of following the Lord, do you think about money and keeping good records as being part of your walk with Him? This verse tells us, the children of God, that we must keep track of our money.

Why does this verse matter? The children of Israel were shepherds and farmers.

The flocks and herds determined their net worth by trading or buying.

In Bible days it was of primary importance that they know the conditions of their flocks and herds. They needed to know any present threats to their prosperity.

This verse instructs us to know the state of our bank accounts, assets, and every aspect of our finances. We need to know our present situation and provide for our future. God wants us to keep track of our money. We need to know where our money is going.

Solomon emphasized that men need to apply themselves to preserve their economic means and to prepare for changes in life that may occur.

People today can get into debt so easily by not keeping good records.

When you wonder where your income is going, that is a good sign that you're not keeping good records. You need to know what you own, what you earn, and what you owe.

Writing down a budget each month will help you keep track of your spending and control your output.

Put on paper what you earn each month and a list of what you owe.

Make a list of what you own—free and clear.

Putting these items on paper will help you acknowledge the changes you need to implement.

God, I thank you for giving me the things that I have. Help me to be more aware and to take responsibility for the state of my finances. Help me to keep good records. Amen.

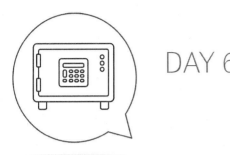

DAY 6

What's in Your Hand?

> *And his master saw that the Lord was with him and that the Lord made all he did to prosper in his hand.*
>
> GENESIS 39:3 NKJV

This verse speaks of Joseph. To perhaps uncover the supernatural in this Scripture on a whole other level for you, let me remind you of a few details about young Joseph's life:

- He was tricked by his older brothers, whom he trusted.

- He was stripped of the special coat his father had given him and left for dead.

- He was separated from his father who loved him; his brothers told his father he was dead.

- He was sold as a slave and lived as a slave.

- He was sold, imprisoned, set up, and lied to.

When Joseph arrived in Egypt, he could have conformed to the ways and customs of the new place and people. He could have abandoned his faith in God, but he stayed the course.

Although Joseph was purchased by Potiphar, he belonged to God.

You need to be the same person wherever you go. Know who you are, who you belong to, and stay true to your roots. Trust God with your life, to keep you safe, to fulfill you, and to bring you to success.

You need to determine in your heart that you will have a good attitude and be Christlike every moment of the day.

In verse 2, Genesis 39 says that Joseph was "a prosperous man." Then in verse 3, it tells us that "the Lord made all that he did to prosper in his hand."

Why? Was Joseph's prosperity coincidence? What was the reason that the Lord prospered him?

When God can trust you, whatever you put your hand to will prosper.

Lord, I ask that like Joseph, you help me not conform to the ways of the world, but that I will stay the course. I ask that whatever I put my hand to, you will cause it to prosper because you trust me. Amen.

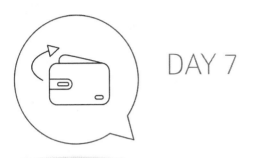

DAY 7

What Do You Want?

> *The Lord is my shepherd, I shall not want.*
>
> PSALM 23:1 KJV

When David wrote this Psalm, he was writing experientially as he was in the role of a shepherd tending sheep.

Daily, David led his sheep to pastures where they could graze and have access to water. He tended to the needs of the sheep. He cared for them.

David was saying here that the Lord is his shepherd, who is in control over his life and provider of his basic needs.

The word "Lord" depicts a person who "has authority, control, rule, or power over others."

As a shepherd taking care of sheep, David was in charge, had control and authority over the sheep he was caring for.

When you make Jehovah God your Lord, you are saying that He has authority and control over your life.

David continued this statement with, "I shall not want." This was a result of his making the Lord his own shepherd. What exactly does it mean to "not want"?

It means that there is no lack of basic needs. The needs for food, shelter, and clothing are all met.

And it means so much more! Our basic human needs for love, belonging, and being cared for are all met in the Shepherd's arms.

Let's confess that the care from my Master Jesus is all I desire. I am content with how He manages my life.

When we make Him Lord, our "personal Shepherd," we allow Him to be the keeper of the gate of our lives and to be in control of every aspect of our lives.

Lord, I ask that I make you my Shepherd. I know that as I do, I won't be in want, and that you are all I desire. I ask that you be the keeper of my life. Amen

---

DAY 8

Trust in Him

> *Trust in your money and down you go! But the godly flourish like leaves in spring.*
>
> PROVERBS 11:28 NLT

The word "trust" in this verse means "to be confident in, to depend upon, to rely on." When we put our trust in money, we are placing our trust in something futile. Money is powerful and can be used for good, but it is tangible and temporal. We know, according to Matthew 6, that we cannot serve two masters. When we try, we end up loving one and despising the other because it is impossible to commit to, love, and give control to more than one entity.

Jesus isn't saying that we can't have money; however, we aren't to place our trust in money. We are to place our trust only in God—the giver of money and all things good.

The person who doesn't acknowledge the power of God will become self-absorbed, trust in themselves and their money. When we don't fear God, meaning reverence or acknowledge Him, we become self-righteous. Without God, we become wasteful because we lose our sense in who we are trusting. Are we trusting in God or are we trusting in ourselves and our own ability?

Folks, this verse brings good news too! When we trust in God, we won't fear circumstances. Trusting in God doesn't mean we can become passive or lazy. It means we rely on God and pattern our lives around His promises. Trusting in God enables us to live by His principles which brings prosperity in all areas of life.

This verse says that a person who puts his trust in God is like a tree that flourishes.

A tree that flourishes is rooted deep in the ground, has healthy roots in good soil, is in just the right amount of sun and shade, is tended to, and produces fruit.

When you place your trust in God, you're rooted in His love, His ability, instead of your own!

Do you want to be healthy in every area of life? Make a decision today to be fruitful, producing what God has entrusted and created you to produce.

Father, I ask that my trust in you will increase. I choose to trust you, because as I do, I won't have to fear any circumstances. I will trust you, which means I am rooted in your love and ability. Amen.

DAY 9

Take No Thought Saying

> *Therefore take no thought, saying, "What will we eat?"*
> *or "What will we drink?" or "Wherewithal shall we be*
> *clothed?" For after all these things do the Gentiles seek;*
> *for your heavenly Father knoweth that ye have need of all*
> *these things. But seek ye first the kingdom of God and His*
> *righteousness, and all these things shall be added unto you.*
>
> MATTHEW 6:31-33 KJV

The words "take no thought" in this passage means "to be anxious, and full of care or worry" are personal characteristics which we should not claim.

Indeed, worry is very real, very personal, and can be a measuring stick that can reveal what is important to you.

In today's Scripture, let's look at the three worries Jesus listed that were common in that day.

1. "What shall we eat?"—Farming was commonplace, and so was the food and crops.

2. "What shall we drink?"—Having enough water was a primary concern because most people lived in wilderness-like domains that could be described as hot, more hot, and most hot.

3. "What shall we wear"—People made most of their clothes, and usually made their own cloth first. Making the cloth, dying the cloth, creating pieces of clothing, and making repairs if something needed fixed were all big deals.

Jesus was saying that although there may be validity to the things we are concerned about, if we will seek Him first, the things we are concerned about will fall into place. He will take care of them.

> **If we seek Him first, the things we are concerned about will fall into place**

The word "seek" is a Greek word "zeteo" which depicts a person that will "search, continue to investigate, and never give up in his pursuit." It's a person who not only inquires, but requires. Requires? Requires what?

When we seek God do we seek Him in such a way that we never give up until we find what the desire of His heart is? Do we set a standard of excellence for ourselves as we live our lives? Do we pursue God and require ourselves to walk honorably every step of the way?

The promise in this Scripture is that our Heavenly Father will ensure that all our needs are taken care of when we put Him first.

Just as worry is a measuring stick of what may be important to you or me, if we're not living uprightly, peace is the measuring stick of what's important to us when we are living in God's will, are at peace with one another, and are full of thanksgiving. (See Colossians 3:1-17 for more insight into this measuring stick of peace.)

Heavenly Father, you know all of my needs. You know every single one of them before I do. Help me to be thankful and to trust you. Your Word is true and you will meet all my needs. Amen.

seek

attempt to find,
desire to obtain
or achieve, ask
for someone

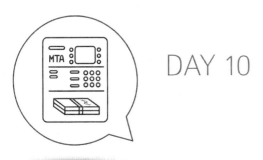

DAY 10

What's in Your House?

> *There is desirable treasure, and oil in the dwelling of the wise, but a foolish man squanders it.*
>
> PROVERBS 21:20 NKJV

One interpretation of this verse can be: "nice and expensive things are in a wise person's home but the fool spends all he earns." The fool, we can then assume, spends money on things.

Today, the principle of saving is like a foreign language to most people. People speak consumerism fluently. Advertisers have tried to convince us of the following self-convictions: "If I want it I'll get it," or "God must want me to have it because it's wonderful like Him."

Have you ever heard these phrases or had similar self-talk going on inside your head?

If so, we can end up spending what we have, what we don't have, and what we could have had later.

Things perish. What doesn't perish? What is so valuable that it lasts forever? Shouldn't we be more apt to "spend" our resources of money, love, and time on those things? What are they?

For a moment, let's look at the word "oil" and "treasure" mentioned in today's scripture focus.

In biblical time oil was a valuable commodity - "liquid money."

The word "treasure" means "cash and valuables." So, the wise man is building up a supply of those things that are valuable which can be spent as cash.

The foolish are referred to as making a lot of purchases and being unwise with their stores and savings, including the money they have on hand.

The wise save and plan for the future. They are watchful not only to consume and enjoy, but they save and make good investments.

The wise save and plan for the future

Saving requires persistence and develops patience and good character over time. Purchases will be more thoughtful and careful. You will not build up or continue to build up waste, so you will have less clutter around you and be more at peace, and better able to work in your surroundings.

You will also have peace because you will be prepared for potential emergencies. You will appreciate the things you have and end up making things last longer.

The foolish man doesn't save, but the wise man saves!

Are you storing away and saving?

Do you spend all that you earn?

What areas can you stop spending?

Lord, I ask that you help me to be a wise person. Help me not spend what I don't have. I ask that you help me to plan and save for the future. Amen.

---

treasure

a quantity of
precious metals,
gems, other
valuable objects,
keep carefully

DAY 11

What Are You Saying?

> *This Book of the Law shall not depart from your mouth, but you shall meditate on it day and night, so that you may be careful to do according to all that is written in it. For then you will make your way prosperous, and then you will have good success.*
>
> JOSHUA 1:8 ESV

The Book of the Law is in reference to the Word of God in us! Why is God telling us to not let it depart from our mouths? Because we are made in His image!

Father God created the world and all that is in it with His WORDS! With us being made in His image, He has given us the power to create with words as well! He is saying that we can create from what comes from our mouths.

The Word of God is to be a constant flow from our mouths. That outflow happens as a result of what we have been thinking. What we think upon is very much influenced by how much we dwell on a thing or the value we place on something or someone, the company we keep, what we're learning and from whom we're learning, the strength of our prayer lives, and the conversations we're having with ourselves in our self-talk.

What we think about all day long will surely show up in our audible conversations and our communications with others

Then, what we think about all day long will surely show up in our audible conversations and our communications with others. The Word will end up coming out of our mouths.

Have you ever thought about a piece of cake? The more you thought about it, the more you desired it. The more you dwelled on it, the more you began to speak out loud about craving cake. You probably ended up having the cake.

Have you ever thought about a business you wanted to start, an investment you wanted to make, or something else you believed God was and is still calling you to be part of to bless Him and others? Has any good fruit been born from these? Is good fruit still being produced?

God is telling us in today's Scripture that as we read, memorize, and meditate on the Word, and just simply think about the Word constantly, the more we will desire it and the more it will come out of our mouths.

Imagine! The Word of God would be dominant in our lives.

When we make the Word dominant in our lives, the result will be that we'll be living prosperously in every area of our lives.

We can't obey the Word if we don't know the Word.

When we study the Word, we understand the Word because Holy Spirit promises to give us understanding and we respond by obeying Him.

Prosperity and all God's blessings are a direct correlation of our obedience.

Have you made a decision to make your way prosperous and of good success? If not, ask God right now to give you revelation by the Holy Spirit to cause the Word to come alive in you. Make a decision today to make the Word dominant in your life. Read it. Think about it. Speak it. Create. Bless.

Lord, I ask that you help me to speak your Word. I will be determined to study your Word, so that I can meditate and speak it out of my mouth. As I make your Word dominant, it will result in being prosperous in every area of my life. Amen.

---

meditate

think deeply,
carefully, and
focus one's mind

DAY 12

Contentment

> *Keep your lives free from the love of money, and be content with what you have.*
>
> HEBREWS 13:5 NIV

This Scripture was written at a time when some people were very anxious about gaining material possessions. These people had property taken from them and their main focus in life was rebuilding their tangible goods, wealth, and estates. Some had crossed the line of reason into loving possessions at any cost.

Is it wrong to seek a better life?

Is it wrong to want nicer things or better income?

Is it wrong to be ambitious and desire an improved lifestyle?

Should we just settle and live paycheck to paycheck without ambition? Is that what content means? No!

Throughout the Word of God, we are taught over and over that wealth is one of God's many blessings. He even tells us to manage the money and possessions He has given us so we can receive more and to discipline ourselves in such a way that we anticipate and plan for our future needs.

The Word also teaches us, however, about the dangers of wealth. In fact, Jesus told the disciples, "It's hard for a rich man to enter into the kingdom of heaven."

So how are we supposed to have contentment when we are to trust Him for our needs?

We are to be content IN Him!

True contentment means we are satisfied with HIM, not with things, possessions, or material belongings.

No matter how much or how little we have, He is the one who satisfies our soul.

He is the treasure that will not rust or fade, break or burn, shrivel or lose its power. Do you have the One Treasure that satisfies above all others?

Lord, I ask that you help me be free from the anxiety of gaining possessions. I choose to be content with what I have because ultimately I need to be content in You! Amen.

DAY 13

Give From the Heart

Give generously to him and do so without a grudging heart; then because of this the Lord your God will bless you in all your work and in everything you put your hand to.

DEUTERONOMY 15:10 NIV

The money we earn through work surely gives us means to be generous at times. Certainly, most people have a desire to help others with all levels and kinds of needs or give to the Girl Scout who comes to the front door with cookies, and absolutely to the bell ringer at Christmas time.

Today's devotional Scripture says that God will bless us in all our work.

Are there ways that we can truly be generous in our work?

This verse certainly seems to say that if we are blessing others with pure hearts then God will bless us in EVERYTHING we put our hands to. We know from elsewhere in his Word that He means in our going to and fro and in waking moments and sleeping times and in our work and leisure.

It speaks of being generous as an aspect of work.

Do you have a co-worker who needs help improving their skill?

This may cost you time and effort. It may even require that you evaluate yourself and question your motives. But, could you be blessing that coworker through your work at work?

This Scripture states that we should give generously, THEN God will bless us!

I think of the widow with just two mites who gave all she had. Certainly, if anyone would have wanted to hold back and not give, it would have been her.

Love motivated her to give, and as a result, she gave everything.

She didn't give it grudgingly and she didn't regret that she gave.

She gave because it was in her heart to give.

Because we give from a heart that's not grudging, God promises to bless the work of our hands.

_____

Lord, I ask as I give, that I will not give grudgingly, but will give because of the love that is within my heart. Help me to always give out of my heart of love, and will result in you blessing my work. Thank you, Lord. Amen.

_____

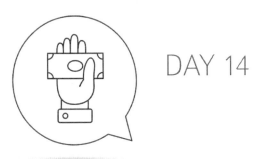

DAY 14

Lend and Rule

> *For the Lord your God will bless you as He has promised you, and you will lend to many nations, but you will not borrow; and you will rule over many nations, but they will not rule over you.*
>
> DEUTERONOMY 15:6 NIV

This is such a wonderful verse of promise. God says that He will bless YOU!

However, some people think that God is willing to bless others but not them. But it says right here in God's infallible Word that He will bless you, me, them, anyone who calls themselves by His name! Say this with me right now, "God will bless ME!" Say it over and over.

It also says "as He has promised you." God ALWAYS keeps His promises. He is not a man that He should lie. He cannot lie.

Has someone ever promised you something and didn't come through?

We never have to think that about God because He says clearly that He will bless YOU!

God always keeps His Word!

"You will lend to many nations," denotes wealth. God is saying this not only as an instruction to not borrow, but He is also saying that you will be so wealthy that you won't even have a need to borrow. You will have so much in abundance that you will be able to lend to others.

In Bible days, when people borrowed and didn't observe the commands of God, they were often carried away as captives.

When they heeded the Word of the Lord, they didn't borrow and they reigned over many nations.

Do you believe that God wants to bless you?

What areas do you want to rule and reign?

Would you rather be a lender than one who borrows?

What steps do you need to take so you can be the lender?

Lord, I ask that you help me become a lender instead of a borrower. I know you will bless me and I ask that you help me make the necessary adjustments so I cooperate with you. Amen.

DAY 15

It's Open

> *The Lord will open for you His good storehouse, the heavens, to give rain to your land in its season and to bless all the work of your hand; and you shall lend to many nations, but you shall not borrow.*
>
> DEUTERONOMY 28:12 NASB

This scripture is so powerful!

The word "open" in this Scripture passage is the Hebrew word "pathach" which means "to open wide, to loosen, appear, break forth, and to unstop."

When something is open, it means there is access to it. God is saying that He has opened His storehouse. Wow!

What is a "storehouse"? It is "a cellar, a treasury, a depository."

Have you ever seen into a bank vault or a bank depository? That is where lenders store large sums of money.

God is saying that He will not only open His depository to us, but He will rain its contents down on us. Praise God!

What is rain indicative of?

Rain is symbolic of refreshing. When the earth is dry and the ground is hard, it is a challenge to grow anything.

When the rain comes down, it refreshes the plants and replenishes the earth so there can be increase again.

Do you need a refreshing today?

God says it's your season and that's when He brings the rain. He will bless the work of your hands.

What are your hands doing?

He will bless the work of your hands.

Lord, I thank you that you open your storehouse to me and that the rains come to my land, so that a refreshing comes to me resulting in increase. I receive your refreshing today. Amen.

Rule or Be Ruled

> *The rich rules over the poor, and the borrower becomes the lender's slave.*
>
> PROVERBS 22:7 NASB

"Why," you ask, "does the Word allow me to commit such an atrocity?" A lender is most likely going to require interest. So the borrower is now subject to the will of the lender and is forced to comply with the lender's terms.

The word "borrower" is the Hebrew word "lavah" which means "to borrow, to cleave, to entwine, and to join."

When we get in debt, when we "borrow," we allow debt to make us slaves. We lose our freedom and independence.

Every time we buy something on credit, charge it, or take out a loan, we start working for the lenders. In other words, we become slaves to the lenders.

The "poor" are poor because they lose money by paying interest. They borrow when they want to spend more than they have.

How many times have you charged something because you didn't have the money in the account to cover the purchase? That's why you charged it.

The wealthy make money work for them through investments. The rich are masters of their money rather than slaves.

God's desire was for Israel to be a creditor, to be able to loan and give rather than borrow.

If Israel obeyed God, He promised that He would make them lenders.

If you have debt today, make a commitment that you will become debt free and become a person who is no longer a slave and in bondage to your finances.

Lord, I ask that you help me not to be a borrower but a lender. I ask that you help me make my money work for me so that I can become debt free and no longer in bondage to my finances. Amen.

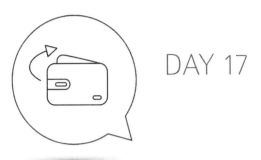

DAY 17

What Should You Owe?

> *Owe nothing to anyone except to love one another; for he who loves his neighbor has fulfilled the law.*
>
> ROMANS 13:8 NASB

The word "owe" means " under obligation, bound by, or indebted to."

Have you ever owed someone something and then struggled to pay it back? How did it make you feel?

I'm reminded of the man with Elisha who borrowed an ax-head and lost it (2 Kings 6:1-7). Their reaction was, "But it was borrowed." Culturally, and from the point of view of integrity, they were startled at this.

What a sinking feeling they must have felt.

In this Scripture, Paul is saying that any debt must be repaid. We are to owe no one because when we owe, it places us in a position of indebtedness. As children of God we are to be free to live victorious lives which enables us to impart victory into the lives of everyone we know if we walk in that freedom.

There's only one thing that we should be indebted to pay, committed to pay, and never be finished paying! What? It is the debt of love!

God is saying we <u>can</u> owe someone something, but the ONLY thing we should owe them is to love.

We can pay debts and be done, and that's wonderful. When we pay back what we've owed and especially when we make that last payment, there is such a sense of relief. We can't say that we are ever done loving, though, ever.

Love should always be what we owe and all that we owe. That's a God-sized goal for us all.

Love should always be what we owe and all we owe

It says in today's Scripture passage that when we love, we are fulfilling the law.

When we love the neighbors (whose pet which does its business in our yard), our acquaintances, co-workers, relatives (with whom we don't get along), we are fulfilling the law ... the law of love.

Jesus said that the commandments are summed up in loving the Lord our God and in loving our neighbors as ourselves.

When we do this, we fulfill the law.

Do a self-check today. How well are you fulfilling the law of love? Do you owe so much money to lenders that you're tied up with working and don't feel you have the time you need to love? What can you do to prioritize love in your walk with God today?

Lord, I ask that you help me to owe no one, but only to love them. Help me to love everyone that I come in contact with. I want to fulfill the law of love and with your help, I will. Amen.

---

owe

have an obligation
to pay or repay
in return for
something received

DAY 18

How to Give

> *Give generously to them and do so without a grudging heart; then because of this the Lord your God will bless you in all your work and in everything you put your hand to.*
>
> DEUTERONOMY 15:10 NIV

The word "give" is the Hebrew word "nathan" which means "add to, bestow, commit, distribute, and to give without hesitation." So we see in this verse that we are to give to others, and we are to also give generously.

We serve the God of abundance. He gave His Son for us, which is the greatest gift.

God doesn't give us "just enough" to get by. He gives abundantly. He gives richly. He goes above and beyond. The Word says that He is such a giver that He will give exceedingly, abundantly, above all that we can ask or think.

We are made in His image, so when we give do we give like God gives? Do we give above and beyond? In fact, if someone asks us to walk a mile, do we ever walk two?

We are to give without grudging? To give grudgingly depicts a person that resents, is grievous, or fearful in giving. Have you ever given something and then regretted giving it because you would then have less? Or have you ever become afraid that what you gave wouldn't come back to you?

When we give like Him, we depict Father God

That is not how God wants us to give.

He wants us to give with a full, abundant heart, without being resentful in our giving.

When we give like Him, we depict Father God and as a result, He says that He will bless all our work and everything we put our hands to.

What are your hands doing?

What work are you doing that you would want God to bless?

Make a commitment today to give more generously and willingly and watch our Father bless all that your hands do!

Lord, I ask that I become a generous person, willing to give without resenting it. I want to be a giver, one who gives abundantly. I choose today to be a giver like you. Amen.

---

give
to freely transfer
the possession
of something
to someone

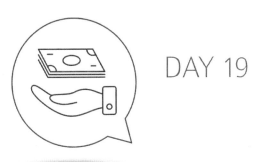

DAY 19

Are You SURE About Surety?

> *A man devoid of understanding shakes hands in a pledge, and becomes surety for his friend.*
>
> PROVERBS 17:18 NKJV

The word "surety" in Hebrew is "arab" which means "to give or be security, as in exchange, engage with, to occupy, or give pledges." You are giving something for security, or exchange, to make a pledge. In other words, a good example would be co-signing a loan for someone. You're making a promise to pay for that person if they default or are unable to pay back the bank. Not co-signing a note is not only a principle of God but also shows good judgment from a relationship standpoint. Generally speaking, you shouldn't co-sign for those you don't know. You co-sign for those with whom you have a relationship. The reason the bank requires a co-signer is because they want to ensure that they will receive their money back.

However, one is never under obligation to co-sign a loan, especially if the one requesting the co-signature is a poor risk.

Before you enter into "surety" with anyone, you'll want to ask some tough questions. You'll want to exercise some "tough love" to save yourself and your family future, unnecessary heartache. For example, has the person been living within their means?

Shaking hands is an illustration of making a promise. Years ago, before attorneys were on every corner, people made promises with a handshake and a word. The handshake was their promise and agreement.

This Scripture is saying that a man who does not have understanding will agree to be the co-signer, or make surety. Get wisdom, friends. Get understanding. Seek it and find it.

Lord, I am committed to not becoming surety for my friends. I am committed to showing good judgment by not co-signing a loan. I ask that you help me in this. Amen.

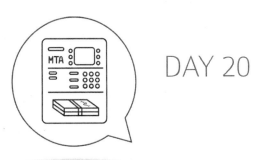

DAY 20

Will of the Heart

> *Then the people rejoiced, for they had offered willingly, because with a loyal heart they had offered willingly to the Lord; and King David also rejoiced greatly.*
>
> 1 CHRONICLES 29:9 NKJV

In the events surrounding today's scripture, David had encouraged the people to give towards the building of the temple. The temple build was a great feat that they had taken upon themselves, one of the greatest known to man yet.

Oh, friends, David was such a generous giver! The Lord most certainly chose a great example in David to show others how to give, but then again, doesn't He always choose the best? David wasn't a perfect man, but he had a heart after God's own heart and that's where it counts! David never gave anything for showmanship, but from love and a sincere heart. His affection was not only for the Lord, but to the house of God.

Because of David's example, the people offered themselves willingly. Isn't it wonderful when we give just because we want to and not necessarily because we are commanded to or because we have to? The people had desired so very intensely to give that they didn't give grudgingly, but willingly. They happily gave offerings, but their hearts had been transformed so they were giving themselves WITH their offerings.

It says that the people rejoiced. The word "rejoice" means "to be glad, joyful, merry and full of glee." They were elated about being able to give what they had, including themselves to the work of building the temple.

> **When we give, it is always a matter of the heart; our hearts show in our giving**

When we give, it is always a matter of the heart; our hearts show in our giving. When you give, do you hesitate or are you excited about what you give?

Do you get excited that you have that item or that amount of money to donate?

Do you give out of duty, or because you are truly happy to give what you have towards God's work?

These are questions we can all ask ourselves to check the condition of our hearts.

Heavenly Father, I come to you in Jesus' name inviting Holy Spirit to illuminate my heart. Show any place that hesitates to give and help me to surrender. You have given your all for me. Help me to never hesitate to give when You ask me to. Amen.

---

rejoice

feel or show great
joy or delight

DAY 21

Honor

> *Honor the Lord from your wealth and from the first of all your produce; So your barns will be filled with plenty and your vats will overflow with new wine.*
>
> PROVERBS 3:9-10 NASB

Webster's Dictionary defines the word "honor" as "to respect, revere, or to treat with submission." When we look at today's Scripture in light of this definition, we see that we need to submit our wealth to God as an aspect of honor. If we say that we honor the Lord, yet we don't tithe and give offerings, then we are deceiving ourselves.

We don't have to be "wealthy" to honor the Lord. The Scripture says that we honor God with our increase or from the "first" of our produce. Have you heard of the tithe? That is the "first" of our produce or wealth. It is the first ten percent that belongs to God. Offerings and giving are beyond the tithe.

What is it that you're producing? Wealth! Every time you go to work, you are trading hours of your life for pay. You are exchanging time, ability, and your expertise for pay. Your income is to not only take care of you and your children, but it's also to help others. If we only have enough to take care of us, then we can't help those around us. We need to make sure we are returning time, expertise, money and goods to the Lord out of honor.

When we honor Him with the first of our "produce," we are saying, "Lord, everything I own is yours. Everything I do I do unto you. Every time I get paid, I am going to honor you because you are my provider!"

Some may think, "I thought my job provided for me." Who gave you that job? Who gave you the ability to work that job? GOD!

God not only requires the first but He deserves the best! God doesn't want our leftovers. In other words, when we get paid and pay some bills, buy some groceries and fill our gas tanks, we shouldn't say, "Well, I don't have anything left to give to God," or "I don't have much left, so I'll give God five dollars." NO! When we get paid, we need to give to God FIRST out of honor. If we don't, we would have to ask ourselves if we truly respect, revere, and submit to Him!

God not only requires the first but He deserves the best!

When we give to Him FIRST, the Scripture says that our barns will be filled and vats will overflow.

The vats and the barns are for storing up, and this is indicative to abundance, or "more than enough."

We serve a God who has more than enough and promises us, His children, that if we will honor Him—respect, revere, submit to His instructions—He will ensure that we are well taken care of.

Lord, I will show honor to you by respecting, revering, and submitting to your Word by giving to you first! Because I do this, you promise me that you will ensure that I will have more than enough to provide for me and my family and that I will be able to give to others who have needs. Amen.

honor

high respect,
esteem

DAY 22

Generosity

> *There is one who scatters, and yet increases all the more, and there is one who withholds what is justly due, and yet it results only in want. The generous man will be prosperous, and he who waters will himself be watered.*
>
> PROVERBS 11:24-25 NASB

God is comparing two different men in this Proverb. One man hoards and holds on to his assets by not giving what he has when he should. Proverbs doesn't tell us why the man chooses to hold onto his belongings and money, whether it's out of greed or fear of not having enough, but clearly the reason does not matter. The man ends up getting poorer and finds himself in want. The other man scatters and sows his money; he gives it out freely and in abundance, yet his prosperity keeps growing and growing.

This man who holds everything back reminds me of a person in today's culture. Many people are concerned about supposed "entitlements" and rights that only exist in the world inside their heads. Many do not have a good work ethic and have a reputation for being "moochy" and lazy, and

God cannot bless mooching or laziness. Stinginess, for any reason, is the other extreme for holding back from giving to others, and God will not bless that either. Being stingy causes a person to hold onto money, assets, skills, talents, and other personal blessings that God blessed that person with for the reason of being a blessing to others.

Laziness, stinginess, fear, or anything that keeps your hand from giving will prevent you from sowing and watering. God has a strategy and He wants us to understand that holding on too tightly to the blessings He has given us will ultimately cause us to be in want. It's one thing to give someone some money, but you need to follow through with expectation. Consider the gift and seed you sow when you help someone. When you plant a seed in the ground, you expect that seed to grow and produce the fruit it's created to produce. That seed needs the right expectation, nurturing, a healthy environment, food, sunshine, and water.

The man who is generous becomes financially prosperous at the same time he is planting and encouraging new life. God blesses the giver.

God blesses the giver The generous and cheerful giver whom God delights in is the one who gives when there's an opportunity to give, whether to the poor, to church offerings, or to a worthy cause, they give more than average. They give above and beyond the need.

When you sow, do you put an expectation on your seed? Do you look at what you have planted to see how it's growing?

Have you known the pull of the Holy Spirit in your inner man to give a gift to someone in need or to a ministry or project, but you held back your gift because you reasoned in your mind that it was too much? Were you afraid?

When you water others, you end being watered yourself.

Father, in Jesus' name, I thank you for the gifts and seed you have given me. I will be faithful with what you have given me and sow and give and because I do, I will increase all the more. I thank you that as I water others, I in turn will be watered as well. Amen.

generous

showing a readiness
to give more of
something, as
money or time, than
is strictly necessary
or expected

DAY 23

Blessed

> *Whoever has a bountiful eye will be blessed, for he shares his bread with the poor.*
>
> PROVERBS 22:9 ESV

The word "bountiful" in this verse means "to be generous." It's referring to a person who not just merely desires to help folks, but to completely relieve them of not having what they need.

He gives generously and is eager to do so.

Why does God bless this kind of man? Because God Himself is the most generous, and He rewards people who glorify Him by being an example of Him to the lost and hurting people here on earth.

God is the One who provides our needs, our desires. So, what we have is all His, or because of Him! How often do we think about our money, assets, time, skills, talents, etc. as belonging to God and existing for His use at His will to bless others? In fact, in Proverbs 19:17, the Word tells us that when we give to the poor, we are lending to the Lord. Certainly, this is figurative, but it's as if we are giving to Him when we give to others.

We are actually saying to God, "Thank you. You can have this back now because you've told me to give it and I know you'll bless us both."

God provided for the poor in the Law of Moses. We see this in Deut. 15:8-10 when God commanded Israel to keep their hearts and hands open to the poor. He promised a blessing upon those who would give.

What is the promise that God gives us when we give to the poor? He will bless us too! Proverbs 11:25 says that the "liberal soul will be made fat."

He promised a blessing upon those who would give

We are promised the blessing of God as we have compassion upon and care for others.

He will deliver us from trouble, He will preserve us!

It says that we will be blessed. The word "blessed" means "made holy, endowed with divine favor and protection."

The Greek definition describes the believer as being "in a position for receiving God's provisions or favor."

Psalm 41:1-3 says, "Blessed is he that considereth the poor; the Lord will deliver him in trouble. The Lord will preserve him, and keep him alive; and he shall be blessed upon the earth."

Generosity guarantees blessings.

Do you look for opportunities to give?

Do you get excited about giving?

What are some ways you can help and give to others?

Lord, I know that everything I have is a result of you blessing and providing for me. I ask that you show me opportunities to give and help others. As you do, I will give out what you desire, knowing that it will be a blessing to others. Amen.

bountiful

large in quantity;
abundant, giving
generously

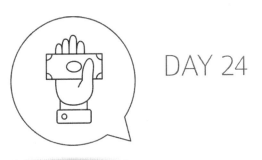

DAY 24

Open Windows

> "Bring the whole tithe into the storehouse, so that there may be food in My house, and test Me now in this," says the Lord of hosts, "if I will not throw open for you the windows of heaven and pour out for you a blessing until it overflows."
>
> MALACHI 3:10 NIV

God is saying to bring the whole tithe, but what is a tithe? The word "tithe" means "tenth," so the tithe is 10% of our income. This verse also instructs us to bring it into the storehouse. The "storehouse" is the local church where you get fed, cared for, and taken care of.

The reason you bring the tithe is so there is "food" in God's house. What "food" is He speaking of? It's spiritual food. In the Old Testament, it is to provide for the Levites. The Levites were the priests of the day that fed the Word to the people.

God also invites us to test Him. This is the only place in Scripture that He invites us to test Him. Why? He wants to prove to us that when we obey with our tithes, He WILL open the windows of heaven over us.

In the King James Version, the word for "windows" as well as a synonym for windows is "floodgates."

See, when floodgates are dammed up, floodwaters may come, but cannot get through the floodgate.

When the floodgate (window) is open, it causes the flood that was sent FOR YOU to get TO YOU!

It means you may get a promotion at your job!

It means you may get that raise!

It means your household appliances, cars and other items last longer than normal! The list goes on!

Father, I will tithe, and as I do I know you have promised that you will open the windows over me. I will be obedient to your Word and as I tithe, your blessings will flow into my life. Amen.

DAY 25

How to Give

> *And He sat down opposite the treasury, and began observing how the people were putting money into the treasury; and many rich people were putting in large sums. A poor widow came and put in two small copper coins, which amount to a cent. Calling His disciples to Him, He said to them, "Truly I say to you, this poor widow put in more than all the contributors to the treasury; for they all put in out of their surplus, but she, out of her poverty, put in all she owned, all she had to live on."*
>
> MARK 12:41-45 NASB

This passage reveals so many wonderful things. After you have had some time with the Lord, ask yourself this question:

Where was Jesus sitting when He commented on the widow's mite?

Hew was sitting in the temple across from the treasury, which is where people brought their offerings.

How differently would we give today if Jesus was in physical form when we gave our offerings?

We see that the rich were putting in large amounts, but there was a widow who put in ONLY two coins. Jesus gave this widow honor for her giving by saying that she had given more than anyone, but why?

How can that be? She gave very little while the rich gave extravagant gifts.

Those who were rich were giving out of their overflow, so they had plenty. What they gave wasn't really a sacrifice. Their giving wasn't sacrificial, but the widow gave ALL SHE HAD! She didn't go back home and have more coins.

We also note that Jesus "observed HOW they gave." What? I thought Jesus saw and recognized WHAT and HOW MUCH we gave. He does, but He not only notes what we give, but the character with which we give it.

See, we can give a lot, but if our heart isn't right, we may as well leave it at home.

If our heart isn't right, we may as well leave it at home

God doesn't want us to give grudgingly and resent or regret what we give. The Scripture says, "God loves a cheerful giver." This is the heart in which we need to give and this is the manner in which the woman with only the two coins gave. Jesus was noting HOW each one gave. How is your "how" today?

*Lord, I ask in Jesus' name that when I give, I'm not just concerned with what I give, but **how** I give. Lord I want to give in the manner of the woman with two mites. I am committed to give with a right heart, not resenting, but giving. Thank you, Lord, that as I commit to this, you will help me. Amen.*

how

in what way
or manner; by
what means

DAY 26

Now is the Time

> *Don't withhold repayment of your debts. Don't say, "Some other time," if you can pay now.*
>
> PROVERBS 3:27 MSG

Being prompt is a valuable principle, not only for repayment itself but of character, as it shows responsibility. The Scripture says, "Don't withhold payment." If you can pay, then pay. You should want to pay off debts as soon as possible. When you get a bonus or extra cash, then pay your indebtedness. Don't go on a shopping spree when you owe money that is due.

When you pay off debts, it builds trust from those to whom you have borrowed. You also have a sense of satisfaction when a debt is paid.

I'm reminded of the story in the Old Testament of the woman with two sons. Her husband was in the school of prophets, but he died! She was desperate, not only because she was in debt, but in those days, if they had no way to pay it, they had to offer their children as slaves to work until the debt was paid in full. God used Elisha, the prophet to do a miracle for her!

The only thing she has was some oil.

Elisha told her to go and borrow as many vessels as she could, and fill all of them up with oil. Although she may not have understood the instruction, she did just that, by faith!

She did as he had instructed her and began to pour, and the oil kept pouring and she was able to fill all the jars.

The Lord multiplied the oil that she had and she was able to sell the oil to pay off her debts! From the value of the remainder of the oil, she was able to live well, and in freedom.

When we do what the Lord instructs us to do, our debts will be paid, and we will be taken care of.

I'm sure that borrowing vessels from her neighbors didn't make sense to the widow, but she did it anyway.

Is God telling you to do something that doesn't make sense?

Are you willing to do what He has said? Do you want to experience a miracle in your finances?

Lord, I am going to pay my debts and I will obey your instruction even if it doesn't make sense to me. Guide me today, Lord, and I will obey. Amen.

DAY 27

Work Method

> *Lazy hands make for poverty, but diligent hands bring wealth.*
>
> PROVERBS 10:4 NIV

We see in this verse that we can choose poverty or wealth! We can choose by our actions or inactions.

Solomon warned against laziness and used the hands to illustrate that.

If we want to be wealthy, we must be diligent and focused.

The word "hands" is, in essence, a figure of speech representing the whole man. Lazy hands represent the man who lacks diligence and is inclined to be idle, negligent, or ignore his responsibilities.

On the other hand (no pun intended), the diligent goes to work early and pursues his job with persistence and focused effort. He is aware that God created him to work and looks forward to working with all his might.

If you work hard, you will be compensated! Daniel was prosperous for over 70 years in the Babylonian Empire, in the midst of a despised people who hated religion. God can cause you to prosper in your place of work, even though it may not be an exemplary environment.

Christians should be the best workers on any job. The world should see us as diligent, hard workers who are persistent to finish the tasks at hand.

God wants to bless His children. It's His desire to bless and prosper you!

Prosperity is a reward of work, perseverance, and effort. If you want to prosper, you must work hard, be disciplined, and determined. When you work hard God will magnify your efforts and put you ahead. He will develop a desire in you to become a goal setter and goal achiever. Do you like to work? Work is good and God blesses those who work hard. Don't go to work late, leave early, and stay on the phone or internet during work hours. Make sure your boss gets his money's worth out of you.

Hard work will create profits in your life and a great feeling of self-worth.

When you work hard and follow God's principles, you will be rewarded!

Lord, I ask that you help me to be diligent. I know that as I work diligently I will be compensated. Even if my workplace may not be the best environment, you will cause me to prosper there anyway. Thank you that prosperity is a reward of work. Amen.

DAY 28

Grace

> *And God is able to make all grace abound to you, so that always having all sufficiency in everything, you may have an abundance for every good deed.*
>
> 2 CORINTHIANS 9:8 NASB

Let's first define the word "grace." In the Greek the word "grace" is "charis" which means "divine influence upon the heart, which gives benefits, favor, liberality and pleasure."

In other words, when the grace of God flows in your life, you will not be in want, because you will be sufficient in everything! God is able because nothing is impossible to Him.

Paul is encouraging the Corinthians to give generously, but he is also aware of who he is talking to. The Corinthians may have been thinking, "If I give, I will be limited," or "If I give this, I won't have enough for myself."

In the previous verse (9:7), he uses an illustration that they would be very familiar with. Using an agricultural metaphor, Paul teaches them that God's economy works differently.

He assures them that their generosity will not cause them to be impoverished.

Paul addresses material things, and abundance in it! Paul says, "... having all sufficiency in everything." Everything!

When we work, when we give, we do not have to fear that by helping others succeed we will compromise our own well-being. On the contrary, God has promised that as we give, He will give us all that we need and more. He assures us that as we help meet the needs of others, He will make sure our needs are met in the process.

Lord, I know that as I give, your grace abounds to me. I know that as I give, I don't end up with less, but I will be sufficient in everything. I am committed to receiving your grace for this day. Amen.

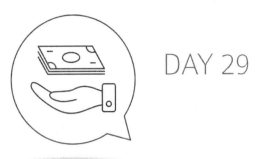

DAY 29

Sow

> *Now He who supplies seed to the sower and bread for food will supply and multiply your seed for sowing and increase the harvest of your righteousness.*
>
> 2 CORINTHIANS 9:10 NASB

This verse says that God gives seed to sowers and bread for food. God says that He will supply extra to those who will sow!

Sowers are ones who use their finances in such a way that they not only see to taking care of their own needs, but they are also found regularly helping meet the needs of people around them. This shows an "other" attitude of the heart.

When you're a sower, God blesses you with an abundance of finances that will not only supply enough to meet your needs, but more than enough so you can help others.

Now, let's consider the fact that most people work to obtain "seed." To most people, seed is their income, the pay for their hard work, the money that helps them provide for their family and show their children and others they look after how to be responsible and take care of the ones God gives them. They're trying to be good examples of being responsible.

Yes, that's all fine and well! We do work so we can pay our bills and provide for our own needs and our family's needs.

We have learned earlier in this devotional, however, that one of the purposes for work is so we can bless others, both for our work itself and by meeting the needs of those outside our comfort zone or our "home stretch."

Some may question me here and ask, "Doesn't God want me and my family to be super blessed all the time?" The answer is YES! The way to blessings isn't trying to meet your own needs, though, but by meeting the needs of others.

What may be hindering some folks' prosperity is that they're eating the bread for food rather than sowing the seed.

If you look at your own assets: home, cars, retirement accounts, 401(k), stocks, etc. and say, "I produced all this," then you haven't tapped into God's source!

As you sow, the seed will increase

When we sow into others and into the Kingdom of God, the Word of the Lord says that He will cause that seed to multiply.

As you sow, the seed will increase and you'll have more to sow!

Lord, my prayer today is that you will trust me with seed and as you do, I will be faithful to sow the seed which you give me. I know that you have blessed me and will continue to do so as I remain faithful. Amen.

SOW

plant, seed by
scattering it on
or in the earth

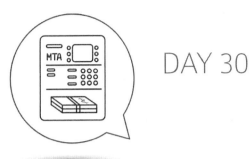

DAY 30

Reap

> *Do not be deceived, God is not mocked; for whatever a man sows, this he will also reap.*
>
> GALATIANS 6:7 NASB

This verse is packed with information. The word "deceived" means "to be led astray, to be led off course or to be affected in such a way that you go in the wrong direction." We certainly don't want to go in the wrong direction, but God is forewarning us to be watchful of this, so we aren't deceived.

Here, it's referring to false teachers leading people away from the truth that will make them free. Paul was speaking to the Galatians, who were hearing false teachers speak about the law of sowing and reaping, teaching that perhaps it didn't work. He was enforcing the importance that we need to give attention to what we believe.

Furthermore, Paul was not only talking to folks that were being deceived, but were also possibly mocking God. He tells us that God cannot be mocked.

The word "mocked" in the Greek, means "to laugh at a person or to even turn a nose up at someone." That is a picture of arrogance!

An arrogant person says, "You are sowing a seed, that doesn't work!"

We have to come to the place that we believe God's Word is true and His Word works.

God is saying that He is not mocked. What He promises in His Word will come to pass!

> **We have to come to the place that we believe God's word is true**

The word "sow" is the Greek word "speiro" which refers to "any seed sown." It refers to love, joy, patience, kindness, and of course, money. No matter what you sow, you will reap it in return. It also depicts a person who continually sows and sows and sows. This is a person who doesn't just sow one seed, but they are continually sowing and sowing and sowing.

If you are faithful in sowing, then you are guaranteed to reap continually.

The word "reap" is of the same present tense, meaning you will reap and reap and reap.

The level that you sow will result in the level that you reap.

If you sow continually, you will reap continually.

———————————————————

God, I am going to sow seed into your Kingdom and as I do I know that you are faithful to your Word and you promise that I will reap. Amen.

———————————————————

reap

cut or gather

DAY 31

Gifts

> *If you then, being evil, know how to give good gifts to your children, how much more will your Father who is in heaven give what is good to those who ask Him.*
>
> MATTHEW 7:11 NASB

In this verse we see several things. God's goodness is being contrasted with men's evil. In other words, if evil men are willing to give good things to their children, then how much more is God, who is good, willing to give good things to His children?

The words "being evil" sound a little harsh, but God is simply reminding us that we are human. We were born into sin and had a sin nature, yet we still knew how to give good gifts to our children.

In James 1:17, Scripture says, "Every good thing and every perfect gift is from above, coming down from the Father of lights." Every good thing we receive has come from our Father God and He is insisting that we ask of Him. We serve a just and good God, and He will give to us not only His grace, His gifts, His abilities, and supply our needs, but He will give to us things that we desire—favor, blessings, and riches.

This calls to mind the story of the prodigal son in Luke 15. The son asks his father for his inheritance early. He squanders it with riotous living and finds himself eating pig slop. He ends up going back home to his father and as he is on his way, his father runs to him and is joyous that his son has returned. His father had already given his son his inheritance and was under no obligation to give any more, but because of his great love for his son, he embraced him and placed a ring on his hand, a robe in his body, and threw a party in his honor.

As a parent, when your children want and desire something, whether it's a toy, a new electronic device, a bicycle, whatever it is, it tugs at your heart and you want to be able to get them what they are asking for. Although children aren't always obedient, or at times squander or don't use the things we give them wisely, we give to them anyway. Even though you may not know exactly how you will make the purchase, you'll do whatever you can to see to it that the gift is given, that the desire is fulfilled. Compare this with God as our heavenly Father. He wants to give us what we are asking for. He is saying, "You know how to give good gifts to your children but I am greater and how much more I will give when you ask."

He wants to give us what we are asking for

God not only will give gifts, but He describes them as good. He will give us what is good for us.

Lord, I come to you now, knowing that you are my Father and help me to understand your heart towards me. Help me understand in a greater way how generous you are. Help me to be generous like you. Amen.

gifts

a thing given
willingly to
someone without
payment; a present

CONCLUSION

As a result of reading this devotional, it is my hope that you have received peace in the area of finances and that you recognize God is the One who supplies all your needs and gives you the ability through work and wisdom to not only rid yourself of debt, but supplies the grace and ability to create wealth.

This book was written for those who have questioned what the Bible says about money, whether or not they can have money, and brief steps for getting out of debt.

KBF MONEY MANAGING

Do you need help eliminating debt, planning cash flow, and building wealth? As a Certified Financial Coach, Karen Ford's money managing techniques will guide you into living debt free. She will help you create and execute budgeting strategies and tackle planning for retirement as you build wealth for your future. Karen offers seminars and coaching for the following:

- keys for debt demolition
- cash flow planning
- how to retire well
- how to build wealth

For information on coaching services, seminars, or to invite Karen to speak, please visit:

www.karenford.org